Aliens and UFOs

CHRIS EVANS

EXCLUSIVE EDITION
SCHOLASTIC
FOR SCHOLASTIC
BOOK CLUBS
AND FAIRS

is there Something out there?

Are we alone in the universe? Does intelligent life exist elsewhere? Are aliens secretly visiting our planet? People report mysterious objects in the sky all the time. Many of them have an everyday explanation, but a few remain unexplained. Could these unidentified flying objects, or UFOS for short, be carrying aliens from other worlds? Only you, alien investigator, can decide!

UFOs AND ALIENS THROUGH THE AGES
For as long as people have walked, they have witnessed UFOs. Take a look at this timeline to discover key moments in UFO history. Find out how reports of UFOs and aliens have inspired science-fiction stories and blockbuster movies. >>>>>>

∧ This photo is taken from the ancient tomb of Ptah-Hotep in Saqqara, Egypt. What can you see?

Ancient mysteries >>>>>>
☿ As long ago as 1480 BC in ancient Egypt, there were sightings of UFOs. Hieroglyphics, or picture writing, from this period describe foul-smelling fiery circles hovering over the court of Egyptian king Pharoah Thutmosis III. Egyptian tomb paintings also show weird creatures with huge eyes that some people think are drawings of aliens from other worlds.

☿ In Australia, 5,000-year-old Aboriginal cave paintings depict spooky giant-eyed beings.

☿ Paintings from 15th-century Europe show weird globes lighting up the sky (see *Ancient Encounters* later in the book).

These ancient mysteries have given rise to the theory that aliens may have landed on Earth. Perhaps the human race itself is descended from aliens. Could we all have alien blood?

∧ Look closely and you can see two hazy balls, or "foo fighters", accompanying this British aircraft.

Wartime spooks >>>>>>
☿ During World War II, aircraft pilots in both Europe and the Far East saw mysterious coloured lights in the sky during their missions. They named these apparitions "foo fighters", after a popular cartoon strip of the time. Sometimes the lights tracked the aircraft or just flew off with astonishing turns of speed. Often pilots fired at the foo fighters, but the objects were too swift to be shot down.

What were these strange objects? Were they ball lightning, as some people have suggested, the hallucinations of fearful pilots – or, perhaps, aliens?

EIA DATA FILE

Greetings EIA agent 7259 – code-name Black. Let's begin your training programme with some key facts.

- It's thought that nearly half of all Americans believe in UFOs
- Up to 70,000 UFO sightings are reported worldwide each year
- More men than women are thought to believe UFOs exist
- Two-thirds of Americans think there is intelligent life elsewhere in the Universe

What do you think? Imagination or reality? Which side are you on, Agent Black?

∧ An illustration of a flying saucer from Kenneth Arnold's own written account of his alien sighting.

Flying-saucer craze >>>>>>

☼ The modern UFO era began in 1947. American airline pilot Kenneth Arnold tracked nine objects moving at high speed in a V-shape over the Cascade Mountains, Washington, USA. He described the objects as silvery and shiny. He said they moved "like a saucer would if you skipped it across the water". Soon newspapers were calling them "flying saucers", and within weeks, hundreds of similar objects were being reported.

☼ In the same year, Harold Dahl spotted five doughnut-shaped craft helping a sixth wobbling UFO in the skies above Maury Island, south of Seattle, Washington, USA. He reported that metal debris rained down on him from the alien craft.

∧ Hot-tempered Colonel Worf is one of four types of Klingon aliens that appear in the *Star Trek* series.

Aliens on screen >>>>>>

☼ In the 1960s, there was an explosion of alien characters in the movies and on TV. Viewers became familiar with the cuddly Tribbles and warring Klingons in *Star Trek*, while thousands of children hid behind their sofas to escape from the death-dealing daleks in the UK TV series, *Dr Who*.

☼ In the late 1970s, the *Star Wars* movies took off. Some of the alien races featured in these movies, such as the bear-like Ewoks and the slug-like Jabba the Hutt, were based on animals from Earth – but they spoke their own languages. Other popular alien movies included *Close Encounters of the Third Kind* (1977) and *ET: The Extraterrestrial* (1982). In *ET*, the gentle alien stranded on Earth learnt to speak English!

∧ This UFO, spotted hovering over Redondo Beach in California, USA, was caught on camera in 2007.

Modern-day UFOs

☼ One recent UFO sighting in April 2007 was reported by English airline pilot Captain Roy Bowyer. "It was a pretty chilling thing," he said. "In many years of experience, I've never seen anything like this. It was extremely pointed, very long and thin. It looked like a CD disc on edge." Captain Bowyer was flying a passenger plane to the Channel Islands, off the coast of France, when he spotted the object. Passengers also witnessed the event. The UFO wasn't captured on film but radar signals confirmed unusual activity in the sky at the time.

Many airline pilots privately tell of UFO sightings, but most never report them for fear of ridicule.

UFO alert!

One December evening in 1996, two men were driving along the Klondike Highway in Canada's Yukon Territory when they spotted a massive object hovering over a frozen lake. Both men watched as the UFO drifted silently across the highway before speeding away. It was bowl-shaped, with a domed top, and ringed with lights. What type of UFO could they have seen?

MIGHTY MOTHERSHIP

The UFO at Yukon may have been a mothership – a giant alien spaceship big enough to carry a whole fleet of smaller craft inside it. In science fiction, a mothership is usually a craft that remains in space and acts as a base station. It provides fuel and other services to smaller, faster-moving UFOs and their crews that head out to explore.

Sightings of motherships are rare. People believe they travel between stars and planets deep in space, so they may only descend into the Earth's atmosphere occasionally. Yet a total of 22 people reported seeing the Yukon mothership. They described it as being bigger than a football stadium and said that it shone a strong beam of greenish light down to the ground!

DISCS, CRESCENTS AND TRIANGLES

More commonly, people report smaller discs, crescents and triangles in the sky. These craft are streamlined in shape, making them well-designed for travelling at speed through our thick atmosphere and for exploring space. Many UFO reports describe fast-moving objects that change direction in an instant. No human-made craft can do this. It would require technology beyond our understanding – and very effective seat-belts for the crew!

"It was a huge ship... Its brightly coloured lights lit up the land around us."
Yukon mothership eyewitness, 1996

< A world of its own

A mothership like this one would need to be a world within itself, with all the conditions needed for the aliens' long-term survival. The inhabitants would need to have fresh supplies, so it might contain gardens where food could be grown and farms for breeding animals. Inside the craft, you might find areas devoted to sports, entertainment and relaxation to keep the crew content. On very long voyages, the mothership may even be a generation starship. This is a place where children are born, raised and trained to take over the running of the craft from their parents.

EIA DATA FILE

EIA agents need to become familiar with the different types of UFOs that could pose a threat to Earth. Memorize these basic shapes for your fieldwork.

Discs and saucers
These craft are classic flying saucers. They are often silver in colour. They may have a domed top and portholes. There are lots of variations.

Spheres and eggs
Spheres and egg-shaped craft appear luminous and glowing. Sometimes they have a ring round them, a bit like the planet Saturn.

Cylinders and capsules
These UFOs are shaped like cigars or airships. They are usually large, with portholes and lights. They move silently through the air.

Triangles and pyramids
Mostly spotted at night, these craft are black with three corner lights. They move at high speeds and are able to turn in an instant.

Chevrons and crescents
These UFOs come in many shapes and sizes. They may be rounded like a sickle or have sharper and more angular curves like a boomerang.

In 1461, in Arras, France, people claimed they saw a fiery iron rod in the sky that was as large as a half-moon. Perhaps this was one of the earliest sightings of a cylinder-shaped UFO.

> In the 1996 film *Independence Day*, a massive alien craft in the sky looms towards Earth, ready to attack. The spaceship was launched from an even bigger mothership higher in Earth's orbit.

Little green men

Aliens may come in all kinds of forms, from little green men and bug-eyed monsters to giant walking lizards and even things that look like talking blobs of pink candyfloss! There are no rules that tell us what an alien should look like, but in eyewitness reports, common features appear again and again.

In January 1967, Betty Andreasson claimed she was kidnapped from her home in Massachusetts, USA, by floating aliens. They beamed a light through her kitchen window and took her to a waiting spaceship.

ALIEN-SPOTTER'S GUIDE

Most people who have encountered aliens describe them as humanoid, or human-like. The most common type of humanoid is the "Grey"; it has a pear-shaped head and large eyes. Other humanoids may be pale-skinned and blond or even have reptilian features. Beings from other worlds may be human-like if the planets where they live have conditions similar to those on Earth. If aliens live in environments that are very different from Earth, they are unlikely to resemble us.

"The beings were small ... with grey skin ... tiny holes for nose and ears, and a slit-like mouth. They gave off a feeling of peace."
Betty Andreasson describing her alien encounter in 1967

< Eerie Greys
Greys are often described as short, hairless beings with pear-shaped heads and large, dark, almond-shaped eyes. They have no visible ears and are usually shorter than a fully grown human. Their slender limbs and large heads suggest a life devoted to mental activities. They usually communicate by "transferring" their thoughts rather than speaking.

> Scaly reptilians
If Earth's reptiles, such as lizards or crocodiles, develop a higher intelligence, they might look like this creature. Reptilian aliens are thought to be cold-blooded (their body temperature changes with their surroundings). They might have webbed fingers and toes, and scaly skin. Like most reptile species on Earth, they could be egg-laying.

AMAZING BODIES WITH A SIXTH SENSE

Another reason why aliens may look like us is because our bodies are efficient. We can walk upright and our hands have grasping thumbs and fingers to pick up objects. Our senses of sight, hearing, touch and taste help us to respond to our environment and warn us of dangers. Aliens might have also developed these capabilities. They might have extra abilities, too. Perhaps some have a sixth sense such as the ability to smell emotions. Or they might be able to project their thoughts into the minds of others and even hear our thoughts.

ADAPTING TO EARTH

Despite sharing some features with humans, aliens are unlikely to be as well-adapted to Earth as we are. They may be used to breathing another type of atmosphere, so they might require special breathing equipment on Earth. Or they might live in a colder or hotter world and need a protective suit. Visiting our planet might not be comfortable for them at all!

∧ The close-up above shows what a reptilian alien's skin might look like.

EIA DATA FILE

All EIA agents must learn to detect the presence of alien life-forms. When investigating potential alien sites, look out for these commonly reported signs:

• Crackling static and buzzing, flickering lights
• Sudden changes in temperature
• Unusual smells, including burning plastic, hot metal and scorched paint
• Charred marks in the ground suggesting the fuel pipe of a spacecraft or landing pads
• A dazed witness with a skin rash or burn marks

ALIENS ON FILM

The alien characters in movies and TV series are often based upon Earth's animals. Friendly aliens may remind us of cute creatures; repulsive ones are based on animals we dislike!

< **Evil mind**
The Borg, in the *Star Trek* series, are part flesh and part machine. They are made up of many different species. Their aim is to conquer and absorb other intelligent races into their "collective" mind.

∧ **Hairy friend**
Chewbacca is a Wookiee and co-pilot of the Millenn Falcon spaceship in *Star Wars*. He communicates by honking.

> **Crime boss**
Centuries-old Jabba the Hutt is a slug-like alien with a slimy manner and unpleasant habits. In the *Star Wars* movies, he controls his criminal empire from a palace on the desert world of Tatooine.

∧ **Deadly alien**
The Xenomorphs from the movie (1979) and its sequels are preda creatures whose aim is to reprod and protect their species at all co

∧ **Not evil, just bad-tempered!**
The Vogons from *The Hitchhiker's Guide to the Galaxy* TV series are a grumpy race who specialize in demolishing planets.

> **"Exterminate!"**
Of the many evil species that have appeared in the *Dr Who* television series, the mechanized Daleks are the best known. They have no emotions except for hate, so they are utterly merciless.

ANCIENT ENCOUNTERS

One of the most spectacular UFO sightings of the past occurred in Germany in 1561. On an April morning the citizens of the town of Nuremberg awoke to a "dreadful apparition". The dawn sky was filled with huge cylinders like cannon barrels, blood-red crosses and globes of various colours. Later, a black object shaped like a spear appeared. All were constantly moving.

FIERY SKY BATTLE

The city's newspaper, *The Gazette*, reported that people witnessed a "frightful spectacle" at Nuremberg. There seemed to be a battle between the UFOs. It raged for an hour. It only ended when some of the globes flew into the Sun and others plummeted to Earth and vanished in a great haze.

> **Ancient depiction**
A woodcut depicting the Nuremberg battle was made by a local artist a few years after the event. What do you think the strange objects in the sky are?

In his 1968 book *Chariots of the Gods?*, Erich von Däniken claimed that alien beings had long been visiting Earth. Not only had they helped to build the ancient Egyptian pyramids, but they had bred with

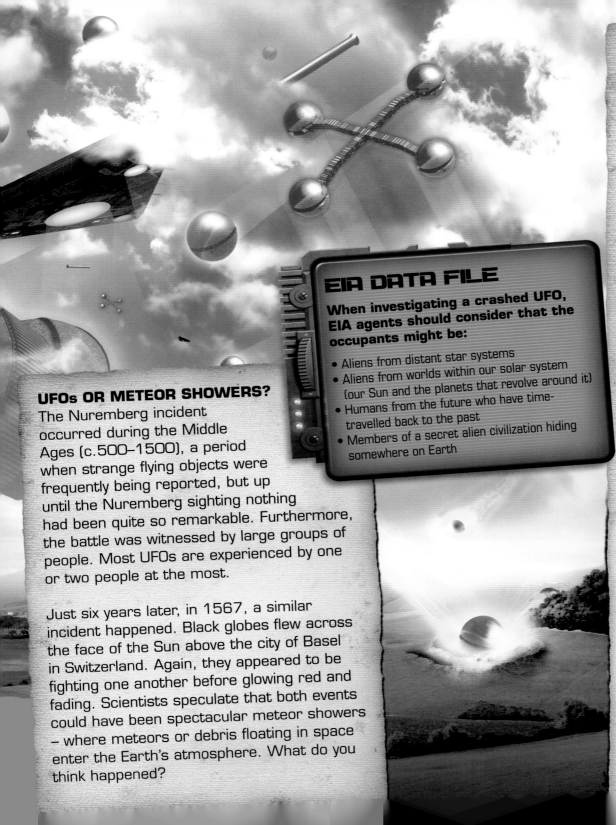

CELEBRITY SIGHTINGS

Many unexplained sightings have occurred in history. The Romans, for instance, reported flaming torches, golden globes and fiery shields that sparkled like fireworks. It was not just ordinary people who experienced UFOs – famous people did, too. These include Greek military leader Alexander the Great and Spanish explorer Christopher Columbus.

∧ **Alexander the Great**
In 329 BC, the army of Alexander the Great was crossing a river when shining silver shields swooped down towards the soldiers, creating panic among men and horses. Several years later, while attacking the Phoenician city of Tyre, Alexander witnessed a glowing beam that destroyed the city's walls.

∧ **Christopher Columbus**
In 1492, Christopher Columbus and a crew member on board his ship, the *Santa Maria*, saw a flickering light that moved up and down in the sky. It vanished and reappeared several times during the night. It was spotted just hours before Columbus sighted land on his voyage across the Atlantic Ocean during his historic exploration of the New World.

EIA DATA FILE

When investigating a crashed UFO, EIA agents should consider that the occupants might be:

- Aliens from distant star systems
- Aliens from worlds within our solar system (our Sun and the planets that revolve around it)
- Humans from the future who have time-travelled back to the past
- Members of a secret alien civilization hiding somewhere on Earth

UFOs OR METEOR SHOWERS?

The Nuremberg incident occurred during the Middle Ages (c.500–1500), a period when strange flying objects were frequently being reported, but up until the Nuremberg sighting nothing had been quite so remarkable. Furthermore, the battle was witnessed by large groups of people. Most UFOs are experienced by one or two people at the most.

Just six years later, in 1567, a similar incident happened. Black globes flew across the face of the Sun above the city of Basel in Switzerland. Again, they appeared to be fighting one another before glowing red and fading. Scientists speculate that both events could have been spectacular meteor showers – where meteors or debris floating in space enter the Earth's atmosphere. What do you think happened?

Alien hunters

If extraterrestrials, or beings from outside our planet, are already visiting Earth, could there also be alien hunters out there trying to track the aliens down? Many people think that governments have teams of dedicated agents to round up aliens before they cause panic on Earth.

BACK TO BASE

Let's imagine that mysterious government hunters really exist and that they carry out scientific analysis on aliens. The base where they operate would be far from prying eyes. The hunters might wear full body suits and helmets with their own air supply to protect them from contamination from alien germs and gases. In this scene, alien hunters are wheeling a trolley of scientific research implements.

MEN IN BLACK

Over the years, some UFO witnesses have reported visits by mysterious strangers wearing dark suits and glasses. Some people speculate that they are government agents trying to keep UFO reports undercover. Or perhaps they are aliens using hypnotic powers to make sure their activities remain secret!

∧ In the film *Men in Black II* (2002), the main characters, agents Kay and Jay, take their roles as government agents one step further. They are charged with ridding the world of evil aliens!

Beakers hold samples of alien fluid for chemical analysis. Some will be used to develop vaccines against alien diseases.

Petri dish holds alien microbes. Investigators observe the microbes to see how quickly they multiply and change.

Portable scanner takes snapshots of alien internal organs and records body temperature.

Microscope helps the investigators to identify skin tissue and dangerous alien microbes, or germs.

Probe is used to explore internal organs and has a heat sensor for recording body temperature.

In 1966, reporter John Murphy claimed he was visited at his radio station in Pennsylvania, USA, by two Men In Black. They wanted to talk to him about photographs he had taken of a glowing object that had crashed in the woods. It may have been a UFO.

ALIEN INTERROGATION

It's likely that alien hunters would interrogate their captives initially to find out where they come from and why they are visiting Earth. Unless the aliens speak the local language, this could be tricky! They might make noises weirder than squeaking bats or howling wolves – we may not be able to decode these sounds! Or perhaps they might produce sounds beyond the range of human hearing.

Even if the aliens could write, we still may not understand them. On Earth today there are manuscripts from ancient times that experts still haven't deciphered. Aliens might not use sounds, symbols or images to communicate at all. They may "talk" in a way that is beyond our human understanding.

EIA DATA FILE

EIA agents should become familiar with the different types of work they may encounter in the course of duty:

- **Gathering intelligence**
  Documenting the hundreds of UFO incidents reported every year
- **Security**
  Protecting secret bases and keeping all activity out of the public eye
- **Investigation**
  Setting up quarantine, or isolation, zones around reported sites of UFO activity to protect people from alien diseases
- **Tracking**
  Tracking and capturing any alien life-forms that are discovered

Utility handpad is an electronic device with several functions. A sensor indicates dangerous levels of any toxic gas, while a translation function can convert alien languages into common Earth tongues such as English. It can also be used as a tracker linked to Global Positioning Satellites. An infrared (heat-sensitive) video camera enables agents to locate runaway aliens at night.

Medicine cabinet contains bottles and cannisters full of all kinds of drugs to protect humans from accidental infection. Alien microbes could be lethal unless the patient is treated immediately.

Ammonia Levels:
65%
DANGER!!

Methane Levels:
0.5%

Alien Translator:
Engaged!

Kidnapped by Aliens

Picture the scene: you're driving along a lonely road late at night. A strange light appears in the sky and your engine suddenly dies. The light becomes a floating spacecraft and slowly lands in front of you. You can hardly believe your eyes! Its crew are human-shaped but they have swollen heads and unearthly eyes. They beckon you inside ...

Did you know that US Presidents Carter and Kennedy, and even Buzz Aldrin, an astronaut on the first Moon landing, have reported UFO sightings?

EARTHLINGS EXAMINED

Why might aliens kidnap humans? Perhaps they are just curious about us or maybe they have darker intentions. Many abducted people say they were examined with strange probes and scanners as if they were part of a scientific experiment. People who say they have been in alien captivity often talk about the experience of "lost time" – hours or even days of missing memory. Sometimes, they suffer from skin rashes or a sensation of being watched. They may not recall the details of their kidnapping until weeks or months later.

UFO

EIA DATA FILE

The US government breaks down encounters with UFOs into different categories. EIA agents should make use of these categories when filing reports.

- **Encounter of the first kind:** person comes within 150 m (500 ft) of UFO
- **Encounter of the second kind:** person sees close-up evidence of UFO such as burnt grass
- **Encounter of the third kind:** person witnesses aliens as well as UFO
- **Encounter of the fourth kind:** person taken on board
- **Encounter of the fifth kind:** face-to-face communication

"They were about 5 ft (1.5 m) tall, had bullet-shaped heads without necks, slits for mouths, and where their noses or ears would be they had thin, conical objects sticking out, like carrots from a snowman's head." **Charles Hickson during a police interview, describing the aliens he saw in 1973**

I MET AN ALIEN ... AND SURVIVED!

There have been many newspaper reports of alien abduction. Here are some of the most famous cases.

Barking aliens

Brazilian farmer Antonio Villas Boas claims to have been kidnapped by blue-eyed aliens who bundled him on board their craft while yapping like dogs. The aliens took samples of his blood and he was forced to breathe a gas that made him ill.
1957

Spooky scanner

Charlie Hickson and Calvin Parker reported being taken on board a domed spacecraft while fishing in Mississippi, USA. Three beings with wrinkly grey skin and crab-like claws grabbed the men, who remember "floating" towards the vehicle. During their visit, Hickson was scanned by a "moving eye".
1973

Alien nightmare!

Twin brothers Jim and Jack Weiner claim that nightmares have led them to remember horrifying events from 12 years before. While fishing with two other men, they encountered a craft and were captured by mind-reading, insect-like aliens who took tissue samples from their bodies.
1988

> Thousands of people go missing every year but most turn up safely. Even if they can't remember what happened to them, very few people claim to have been kidnapped by aliens. But perhaps they just don't know!

The Hill Abduction
(also known as the Zeta Reticuli incident)

On the evening of September 19, 1961, Barney and Betty Hill were driving along a deserted mountain road in New Hampshire, USA, when a bright object in the sky suddenly dropped down towards them. Barney watched it through his binoculars, and was astonished to see several humanoid figures in the window of a strange craft. The Hills drove home as fast as they could.

Betty and Barney Hill with a drawing of the UFO they witnessed.

Over the following five nights, Betty dreamt a different version of the story. In her dream, short, hairless beings with large foreheads had taken the Hills inside a spaceship and subjected them to a medical examination. Betty described the aliens as pleasant. She asked the leader where he came from, and he showed her a map of a star system but it was meaningless to her.

During the summer of 1962, doctors put Barney and Betty under hypnosis, in separate rooms, to see if they could recall anything else. Betty sketched the star map she had seen, explaining that the connecting lines were trade routes between the stars. Under hypnosis, Barney told exactly the same story as Betty's disturbing dream.

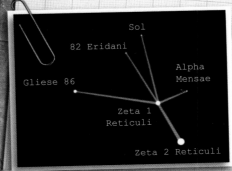

In 1968, an amateur astronomer matched Betty Hill's star map to the double star system Zeta Reticuli, but other astronomers disputed the match. The verdict on the case is left open.

JAKE FM

A Saucerful of Secrets

Imagine you have sneaked on board an intergalactic spaceship. The craft is a product of advanced alien engineering. It's far faster and easier to manoeuvre than any aircraft on Earth. It can race across space or hover silently over the ground. Take a good peek around.

Captain's refreshments include venom milked from alien snakes – fatal to a human!

Joystick is floating and can be altered a full 360 degrees to change the ship's path in micro-seconds. Its organic, skin-like covering contains thousands of sensors that make it sensitive to the slightest touch.

Hyperdrive – push this lever to move from cruising speed to faster-than-light travel. In hyperdrive mode, the spaceship emerges instantly at its destination as if travelling through a black hole.

EIA DATA FILE

Get to know these advanced methods of deep-space travel:

- **Flight through a wormhole:** a wormhole is a loop or "hole" in space and time that connects distant points in the universe. A starship entering one end of a wormhole would emerge at the other end having travelled a vast distance in seconds.
- **Journey through a stargate:** a stargate is similar to a wormhole but is an artificial structure built by alien civilizations for swifter travel.
- **Warp drive:** using an on-board warp drive, a spaceship can shrink or "fold up" space and time so that journey times are dramatically reduced.

Light travels faster than anything we know. A ray of light can travel from the Earth to the Moon in just over one second. To cross our galaxy at light-speed, it would take 100,000 years!

Inertia damper protects the crew from crushing gravitational forces (g-forces) when the pilot rapidly increases speed or changes direction.

Friction absorber channels the heat caused by friction when the spaceship travels through space. Without the absorber the craft may burn up.

Holographic intercom is used by the crew to speak privately to members in other sections of the ship. A holographic (made with a laser) image of the person you are communicating with appears above the intercom.

Ship's mascot – as well as making the alien crew feel at home, this furry pet honks loudly at changes to onboard conditions, alerting the crew to the danger.

Human tongue carpet is a living floor with the rough moist texture of a human tongue. Naturally warm, it also ripples under the crew's feet.

Spaceship's computer is linked by electro-nerve bundles to the pilot so that the alien and the craft are one being. This ensures that all commands are carried out instantly.

alien activities

It's 3 a.m., December 26, 1980. A UFO is spotted close to military airbases in eastern England. A security patrol sees flashing lights between the trees in nearby Rendlesham Forest. It hears noises that sound like animals screaming. Then, in a clearing, the patrol spots a cone-shaped object shrouded in yellow mist. What are these strange alien activities in the woods?

EIA DATA FILE

All EIA agents should fill out a UFO investigation checklist at the site of an extraterrestrial encounter. Evidence reported may include the following:

- Scorched or flattened vegetation with marks in a regular pattern suggesting the presence of a UFO
- Animal disturbances such as dogs barking and howling
- Electrical interference on car radios
- Confused and disorientated witnesses with memory loss or missing companions
- Minor injuries to witnesses such as small marks and blotches on skin, possibly due to examinations by aliens

IF YOU GO DOWN TO THE WOODS TONIGHT ...

Staff Sergeant Jim Penniston was one of the members of the Rendlesham patrol. He recalled the UFO as being "black in colour with lighting running through the fabric of the craft". Describing the encounter, he said: "After 45 minutes it powered up and went to tree level and took off. No sound, no air displacement." Airman John Burroughs accompanied Penniston. This was his description: "It had a bank of blue lights on it and it was sitting there ... When it was happening, everything seemed to go slower. Everything felt different. When it disappeared, everything seemed normal again."

TWO NIGHTS LATER

The deputy base commander, Lieutenant Colonel Charles Halt, took a second patrol out and spotted flashing red lights in the sky. He explained: "I saw something that was oval-shaped, had a black centre and appeared to be dripping something like molten metal off it. It moved horizontally through the trees, occasionally bobbed up and down. It came towards us at one point. It moved out across a field. The object was illuminating a farmer's house beyond us. Suddenly the object just exploded into five white objects and it disappeared."

No one ever found physical evidence of the UFO but broken branches and indentations in the ground were spotted. The Rendlesham Forest incident remains a mystery to this day. Witnesses insist they saw something strange but the official version is that nothing unusual happened at all.

ASK THE PANEL

Is the Rendlesham Forest story just one more piece of evidence that aliens are visiting our Earth? If so, why might aliens want to come here? Perhaps they are just curious about the strange, sociable species called humans, or maybe they feel they can learn from us – or they could be planning to take over! Take a look at what our UFO panel thinks. Who do you agree with?

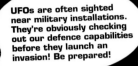

UFOs are often sighted near military installations. They're obviously checking out our defence capabilities before they launch an invasion! Be prepared!

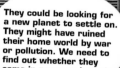

They're mischief makers. Crop circles, ghosts, fairies, the Bermuda Triangle – I blame them all on aliens!

They could be looking for a new planet to settle on. They might have ruined their home world by war or pollution. We need to find out whether they come in peace or intend to overthrow us.

They're kidnapping our people to perform evil experiments on them! Stay inside! Lock all your doors! Keep watching the skies – just in case!

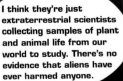

I think they're just extraterrestrial scientists collecting samples of plant and animal life from our world to study. There's no evidence that aliens have ever harmed anyone.

Crop circles

In the 1970s, mysterious patterns of flattened vegetation appeared in farmers' fields worldwide. They were given the name "crop circles" and they became more elaborate as time went on. Many people believed they were evidence of alien activity – until mischievous humans owned up to having created them.

∧ In the 1977 film *Close Encounters of the Third Kind*, witnesses stand entranced and rooted to the spot as a glowing UFO lands in front of them to deliver home humans who were taken on board the UFO years before.

are they... among us?

Have you ever met a real alien? Some people believe that aliens are already living secretly on Earth, researching our planet. Perhaps there are aliens in disguise in a café just down the road from you!

NOW YOU SEE ME...

Even humanoid aliens are unlikely to look exactly like human beings. They might have slightly different skin or strange eyes. Some aliens might be shape-shifters, taking on the appearance of anything near them. Others might wear a device that projects a human-like image. Or they may wear an invisibility screen so they can't be seen at all!

Aliens at large

Look carefully at this scene of a busy café. Can you spot the tell-tale signs that extraterrestrials might be at large? Perhaps they have gathered in the café to hold a meeting between members of advanced races that have been exploring Earth. How many aliens can you find? Remember, some of them won't look remotely human! You'll find the answers upside-down at the top of the opposite page.

EIA DATA FILE

EIA agents should be alert to the tell-tale signs of aliens in disguise:

- A human appearance but a shadow that takes a non-human shape
- A shimmering or blurry body outline
- A high- or low-pitched voice, possibly talking in an unknown language
- Odd movements, such as jerky strides, and double-jointed knees or elbows
- Peculiar mannerisms, such as the licking of armpits, pulsating nostrils and twisting heads 360 degrees

Some scientists believe that tiny invaders from Mars are already here! Fragments of rock, called meteorites, that fell to Earth in Egypt and Antarctica may contain Martian bacteria.

ANSWERS (FROM LEFT TO RIGHT)
Back table: man has a webbed hand
Front left table: child has an alien in his T-shirt pocket; man is reading an alien newspaper and has strange eyes
Counter area: plant is an alien species; chef has an alien shadow; drink on the games machine has arms
Front right table: man has a serpent tongue; ice-cream has an eyeball; woman has five-fingered hands

THE SMELL OF ALIENS

Could it be that you can recognize an alien from its smell? Aliens that breathe the following gases in the atmospheres of their home planets might give themselves away by these distinctive odours:

- Ammonia: an odour of smelling salts
- Chlorine: a swimming-pool whiff
- Hydrogen sulphide: the stink of rotten eggs
- Sulphur dioxide: a choking smell

SECRET SITES

Have UFOs ever crashed on Earth? Have aliens been taken to secret sites for examination? Do the authorities cover up these stories? Many people believe that the US government has secret, maximum-security locations where teams of scientists are on standby to investigate aliens and spacecraft remains. This is what a secret site might look like.

CRASH-SCENE INVESTIGATIONS

What could be happening at these secret sites? If investigators have found alien corpses in UFOs that have crashed, they might be carrying out medical examinations to uncover the differences between humans and aliens. An examination could reveal many things, from what kind of gases the aliens breathed on their planet, to what they ate just before they died. Investigators might also "reverse engineer" damaged UFOs, or take them apart to see how they work. The investigators may even rebuild them. There have been several reports of experimental craft flying over secret areas – perhaps the military are trying out alien spacecraft!

EIA DATA FILE

To deal with any type of alien encounter, pack the following items in your EIA kitbag:

- Taser (stun) pistol with "immobolize" and "knock-out" modes
- Sonic concussion grenades
- Visor with anti-glare and infrared night vision
- Electromagnetic net for capturing energy beings
- Helmet with poisonous gas detector
- Protective body suit, resistant to all fluids

THE MYSTERY OF AREA 51

A top-secret military airbase located in the Nevada desert, USA, is the source of many UFO rumours. Area 51, as it is known, is run by the US Air Force. It specializes in developing new military aircraft. Shrouded in mystery, some people speculate that alien craft have been tested there and that secret meetings with extraterrestrials have even taken place!

RESTRICTED
AUTHORIZED
PERSONNEL

In 1974, astronauts aboard the Skylab 4 space station got into trouble for taking satellite photographs of restricted areas in the USA. They explained that they had made a mistake!

ARMY REVEALS FLYING DISC

There is a famous story of a UFO crash that took place in 1947 in New Mexico, USA. It began when a farmer reported that he had found some unusual materials on a ranch about 112 km (70 miles) from the Roswell Army Air Field. Shortly afterwards, the army issued a statement revealing they had found a flying disc. Later, they took back their statement, claiming that the materials were the remains of a scientific weather balloon.

However, the story would not go away. Other witnesses insisted that a UFO crew had been taken to the Roswell base. They said examinations were carried out on alien corpses. Nothing has ever been proven but the Roswell incident remains one of the most notorious UFO cases of all time.

∧ Real or fake?
Some people claim that a scorched body of a dead alien was found at Roswell, USA, in 1947. Others say the story was a hoax. This is a model of an alien corpse from the International UFO Museum at Roswell.

< Weather balloon or UFO?
This photo shows pieces of a weather balloon that the military claim fell to Earth near Roswell at the same time. Other people say that the strange materials discovered were parts of a UFO. What do you think?

Can you speak ⬚⬚⬚⬚⬚?

Let's imagine that investigators have captured an alien who communicates by changing the patterns in its eyes rather than by making sounds. The team have studied the alien for many months and have finally learnt how to translate the meaning of each eye pattern.

⬚ = A	⬚ = J	⬚ = S
⬚ = B	⬚ = K	⬚ = T
⬚ = C	⬚ = L	⬚ = U
⬚ = D	⬚ = M	⬚ = V
⬚ = E	⬚ = N	⬚ = W
⬚ = F	⬚ = O	⬚ = X
⬚ = G	⬚ = P	⬚ = Y
⬚ = H	⬚ = Q	⬚ = Z
⬚ = I	⬚ = R	

Using the alien language decoder above, see if you can translate the other-worldly conversation below that took place at the imaginary secret base.

CONVERSATION WITH AN ALIEN

Investigator: Who are you?

Alien: ⬚ ⬚ ⬚⬚⬚

Investigator: Where do you come from?

Alien: ⬚ ⬚⬚⬚⬚⬚ ⬚⬚⬚⬚⬚

Investigator: Why are you here?

Alien: ⬚ ⬚⬚⬚⬚ ⬚⬚ ⬚⬚⬚⬚

Investigator: What do you want?

Alien: ⬚⬚⬚⬚⬚ ⬚⬚⬚ – ⬚ ⬚⬚⬚⬚⬚

Investigator: Why are your nostrils twitching?

Alien: ⬚⬚⬚ ⬚⬚⬚⬚⬚ ⬚⬚⬚⬚⬚⬚, ⬚⬚⬚⬚

weird worlds

Imagine a world where giant volcanoes spew out molten lava and gases fill the air with the stench of rotten eggs. In the sky, twin suns have risen, bathing the fiery landscape in a fierce light. The surface temperature is 80°C (176°F) – near boiling point. On this planet, it's just another perfect summer's day ...

UNDER AN ALIEN SKY

What might intelligent life be like on another world? This imaginary scene shows a planet where an alien civilization has developed. The beings living here have a tough reflective skin that reflects back the sun's hot rays, but they also spend time indoors to escape the heat. Their slender bodies suggest that the gravity on this planet is lower than on Earth, allowing their limbs and necks to grow extremely long.

Some scientists believe that advanced life can develop only on Earth-like planets where there is a warm temperature, water and oxygen. But others disagree. It's possible that life could develop in the most unlikely places. Maybe an alien race is living on a freezing moon in another galaxy or on a planet whirling around an energy-sucking black hole.

EIA DATA FILE

Check out these terms from the EIA Astronomical Dictionary and become familiar with objects in our known universe.

- **Black hole:** the super-compressed remains of a star. Its gravity is so powerful it can even suck in light.
- **Exoplanet:** a planet outside our solar system orbiting a star other than the Sun.
- **Gas giant:** a large planet with a dense gaseous atmosphere, like Jupiter, and probably no solid surface.
- **Moon:** a natural body in space that orbits another planet. Thirteen moons circle the planet Neptune.

∧ **Alien planets**
The landscapes of planets vary depending on the type of gases that are in their atmospheres, their weather conditions and how near they are to the star they orbit. Planets can be fiery hot or icy cold, in constant daylight or in pitch blackness. Thunder storms might be raging and ferocious winds blowing night and day.

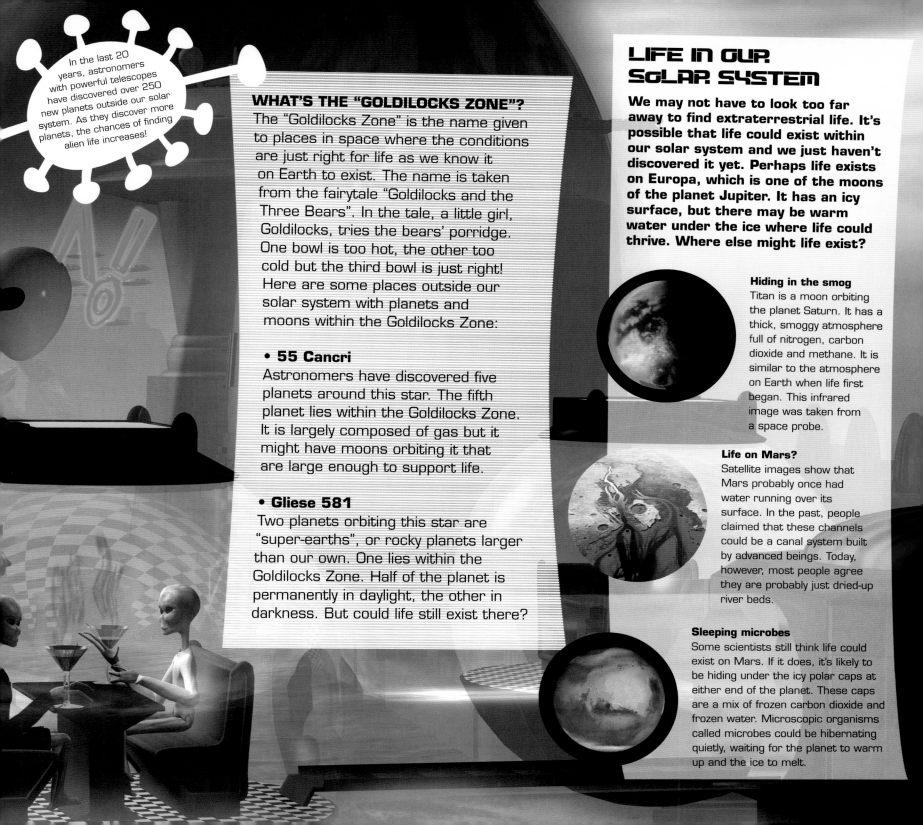

In the last 20 years, astronomers with powerful telescopes have discovered over 250 new planets outside our solar system. As they discover more planets, the chances of finding alien life increases!

WHAT'S THE "GOLDILOCKS ZONE"?

The "Goldilocks Zone" is the name given to places in space where the conditions are just right for life as we know it on Earth to exist. The name is taken from the fairytale "Goldilocks and the Three Bears". In the tale, a little girl, Goldilocks, tries the bears' porridge. One bowl is too hot, the other too cold but the third bowl is just right! Here are some places outside our solar system with planets and moons within the Goldilocks Zone:

• 55 Cancri

Astronomers have discovered five planets around this star. The fifth planet lies within the Goldilocks Zone. It is largely composed of gas but it might have moons orbiting it that are large enough to support life.

• Gliese 581

Two planets orbiting this star are "super-earths", or rocky planets larger than our own. One lies within the Goldilocks Zone. Half of the planet is permanently in daylight, the other in darkness. But could life still exist there?

LIFE IN OUR SOLAR SYSTEM

We may not have to look too far away to find extraterrestrial life. It's possible that life could exist within our solar system and we just haven't discovered it yet. Perhaps life exists on Europa, which is one of the moons of the planet Jupiter. It has an icy surface, but there may be warm water under the ice where life could thrive. Where else might life exist?

Hiding in the smog

Titan is a moon orbiting the planet Saturn. It has a thick, smoggy atmosphere full of nitrogen, carbon dioxide and methane. It is similar to the atmosphere on Earth when life first began. This infrared image was taken from a space probe.

Life on Mars?

Satellite images show that Mars probably once had water running over its surface. In the past, people claimed that these channels could be a canal system built by advanced beings. Today, however, most people agree they are probably just dried-up river beds.

Sleeping microbes

Some scientists still think life could exist on Mars. If it does, it's likely to be hiding under the icy polar caps at either end of the planet. These caps are a mix of frozen carbon dioxide and frozen water. Microscopic organisms called microbes could be hibernating quietly, waiting for the planet to warm up and the ice to melt.

searching for extraterrestrials

The writer Arthur C Clarke has suggested that alien races might be mining or stars for raw materials or using them as an energy source. If so, exploding stars, called supernovas, could be the cosmic equivalent of factory accidents!

We have no firm evidence that aliens exist, but how can we be sure they don't? They may be trying to contact us. SETI – the Search for Extraterrestrial Intelligence – is an international project that involves scanning space with giant radio telescopes in the hope of discovering an alien race. The scientists work with radio telescopes rather than optical telescopes because radio waves from distant sources are easier to detect than light.

WHERE ARE THEY?

Why haven't we discovered any alien signals so far? One theory is that truly advanced races might be using energy sources we can't presently detect. Or they might now be living inside a Dyson sphere. This is a giant hollow shell built by an alien nation surrounding their star to ensure their long-term survival. The Dyson sphere would capture all of the star's energy, so none of it could be detected by radio telescopes on Earth.

HUMANS ON ALIEN TV

Any advanced civilization should eventually make its presence felt. For over 60 years, television signals from Earth have been leaking out into space. If aliens do exist on distant worlds, they may just be receiving our earliest TV shows. Perhaps now, they will get in touch!

IS ANYONE OUT THERE?

In August 1977, Dr Jerry Ehman was part of a team monitoring space signals from the Big Ear radio telescope in Ohio, USA. Checking a computer print-out, he spotted a signal burst so striking that he ringed it with red pen and beside it scribbled: "Wow!"

The Wow! signal remains unexplained. Was it a brief intense message from an extraterrestrial civilization? Scientists had been searching for a message like this for decades. Since the event they have rechecked the region of space where the original signal may have come from. Nothing like it has been recorded since.

∧ This facsimile shows radio frequencies recorded by the Big Ear telescope. The one-off "Wow!" signal is marked in red.

∧ **Pioneer 10**
The Pioneer 10 space probe has been travelling for over 35 years. It has left our solar system and is deep in space. Scientists made faint contact with it for the last time in January 2003.

EIR DATA FILE

What are the chances of intelligent life existing elsewhere in our galaxy and how will we be able to communicate with it? Scientists say this depends on:

- How many stars have orbiting planets where aliens could live
- How favourable the conditions are on these planets
- The chance of life forms acquiring a higher intelligence
- The number of civilizations sending signals or craft into space
- The length of time these civilizations send signals or craft into space

∨ The golden plaques on the Pioneer 10 and 11 space probes show human figures and a diagram of Earth's place in the solar system.

GREETINGS FROM EARTH

In 1972 and 1973, scientists launched the Pioneer 10 and 11 space probes to explore the solar system. Although the main purpose of these unmanned craft is to investigate the outer planets, they also carry plaques giving information about Earth. This is just in case they run into extraterrestrial life who are interested in our planet!

If they come

Imagine alien spaceships suddenly appearing in the skies over our major cities and military installations. Entire fleets could materialize from deep space in an instant. Such an abrupt arrival would almost certainly cause mass panic, but would the aliens be hostile or would they come in peace?

Aliens could threaten our existence by bringing in microbes, which might carry diseases. Humans might have no resistance to these diseases and the whole human species could be wiped out!

INVADING OUR SPACE

Why might aliens want to invade Earth? Perhaps they wish to settle on our planet, so exterminating the local population and razing its cities would be necessary to clear the ground for their new civilization. Or they might want to farm the Earth, using enslaved humans to harvest their crops and serve as drones!

MIND PARASITES AND BODY SNATCHERS

Another possibility is that an alien invasion could be carried out secretly. Extraterrestrials might be able to project themselves into human brains and take control of our bodies. In this way, they could occupy Earth without a battle. Living inside a human skin would also mean they could survive on our planet with ease.

Alien attack

In the 2005 film, *War of the Worlds*, a hostile alien invasion threatens to destroy the Earth. The long-legged tripods vapourize everything in their path. They are only defeated when they catch a deadly human virus.

TAKE ME TO YOUR LEADER

Perhaps alien visitors would come in peace. Many scientists argue that a civilization more advanced than ours will have conquered its aggressive instincts and urge to destroy. Their arrival on Earth could be a sign that the human race is now considered developed enough to face up to the startling news that it is not alone in the universe.

GALACTIC GREETINGS

Peaceful aliens might visit for several purposes. They could be concerned that the human race is in danger of destroying itself and its planet, so they might arrive to offer help or guidance. Alternatively, these aliens may have decided we are ready for the next stage in our development – to join the galactic equivalent of the United Nations! The United Nations is the international organization that promotes cooperation between Earth's nations.

EIA DATA FILE

EIA agents must respond with appropriate actions for any threats by a UFO. These are:

THREAT: UFO flying over thinly populated area
REASON: Sightseeing or terrain-mapping
ACTION: Track craft until it disappears

THREAT: UFO buzzing land vehicles
REASON: Alien joyriders and mischief makers
ACTION: Fire warning shot to disperse UFO

THREAT: UFO flying over military installation
REASON: Gathering intelligence
ACTION: Aerial response to scatter intruders

THREAT: Full-scale UFO attack
REASON: Destruction of the human race
ACTION: Mobilize all armed forces and agents

They come in peace
The film, *ET: the Extraterrestrial*, from 1982, portrays a lovable young alien stranded on Earth when his spaceship leaves without him. ET makes friends with a human family that helps him to return to his native planet.

EIA AGENT TEST!

To be a top-level EIA agent you must be an expert in ufology – the science of aliens and UFOs. Take this EIA agent passing-out test, then check the answers (shown upside-down at the bottom of the opposite page) to discover what grade you have achieved. Read each question carefully and choose the correct the letter. You can find all the answers to the questions in the book. Good luck!

date: 03/03/
them again

PART 1 ALIENS AND SPACESHIPS

Q1: What does UFO stand for?
A) Unfamiliar Flying Object
B) Unexplained Fast Object
C) Unknown Floating Object
D) Unidentified Flying Object

Q2: When was the word "flying saucer" first used to describe a UFO?
A) 1847
B) 1947
C) 1974
D) 1997

Q3: What is a mothership?
A) a spacecraft big enough to contain smaller craft
B) a UFO with a crescent shape
C) a shining UFO
D) a weather balloon that has been mistaken for a UFO

Q4: Which description best fits an alien Grey?
A) scaly head, green eyes, hairy body
B) pointed head, no eyes, hairless body
C) pear-shaped head, large eyes, hairless body
D) tiny head, red eyes, scaly body

Q5: Which of these is NOT a common symptom of people who are abducted by aliens?
A) experiencing memory loss and "lost time"
B) suffering from skin rashes
C) vivid nightmares involving medical examinations
D) developing a cough and twitching eyelids

Q6: What might a hyperdrive be for on a spaceship?
A) increasing the atmospheric pressure on the bridge
B) allowing the craft to travel faster than light
C) converting excess heat into energy to power the craft
D) protecting the crew from crushing g-forces

Q7: Which of these alien characters did NOT appear in the *Star Wars* films?
A) Chewbacca
B) Ewoks
C) Xenomorphs
D) Jabba the Hutt

Q8: What is a humanoid alien?
A) an alien from the planet Hybridia
B) an alien that has similar features to a human
C) a super-intelligent alien
D) a human with superpowers

Q9: What does it mean to "reverse engineer" an alien spacecraft?
A) to build a UFO that flies backwards
B) to build a UFO that can go back in time
C) to sabotage a UFO so that it can't fly
D) to take a UFO apart to see how it works

Alien type: Grey. Four sightings!

0000083737272839494

Sample: MJ.D 05/11/74
radiation level: 10.9%

02 8 88 00111 001

AREA 51
passcard